EMPHYSEMA
A Love Story

EMPHYSEMA
A Love Story

JANET MUNSIL

NUAGE
EDITIONS

Cover design by Terry Gallagher /Doowah Design.
Photograph of Janet Munsil by Joan Wade.
Cover photograph of Ravonna Dow by Trudie Lee.
Published with the assistance of The Canada Council for the Arts and the Manitoba Arts Council.
Printed and bound in Canada by Veilleux Impression à Demande.

Canadian Cataloguing in Publication Data

    Munsil, Janet
        Emphysema : a love story

    A play.
    ISBN 0-921833-71-7

    I. Title.

PS8576.U576E56 2000   C812'.54   C00-900383-5
PR9199.3.M824E56 2000

Nuage Editions, P.O. Box 206, RPO Corydon
Winnipeg, MB, R3M 3S7

To My Dad

Emphysema was first produced by Alberta Theatre Projects, D. Michael Dobbin Producing Director, as part of Pancanadian playRites '97. The cast was as follows:

Ken   David Schurmann
Lulu   Ravonna Dow
Louise Shelia Moore

Directed by Micheline Chevrier
Set Design by Helen Jarvis
Costume Design by Judith Bowden
Composer Alan Rae
Lighting Design by Brian Pincott
Stage Manager Colin McCracken
Assistant Stage Manager Gina Moe

Emphysema was developed in workshop and presented at the Belfry Theatre's Studio Series in 1996. The cast was as follows:

Ken   Paul Terry
Lulu   Abigail Kitt
Louise   Margaret Barton
Pianist Stephen Hatfield

Directed by Tim Crofton
Set and Costume Design by Paul Dishaw
Lighting Design by Ian Rye
Production Coordinator Kate Wallace

An earlier version of *Emphysema* was presented at the Open Space New Theatre Series in 1995, directed by Tim Crofton and with Paul Terry as Ken and Florence MacGregor as Louise/Lulu. The Stage Manager was Justine Thompson.

ACKNOWLEDGEMENTS
The author wishes to thank: Paul Terry, Kevin Bazzana, Mark Dusseault, Micheline Chevrier, Lynn Spink, Alan Powell, Tim Crofton, Stephen Hatfield, Alberta Theatre Projects, the BC Arts Council, Playwrights Theatre Centre, Glynis Leyshon, Jennifer Lord, Mary Desprez and the Belfry Theatre, Tracey Wait, Urjo Kareda, Open Space, Vic Mitchell, Robert Astle, Margaret and Satan Barton, Alice Bacon and John Carswell, Florence MacGregor, Abigail Kitt, David Schurmann, Sheila Moore, and Ravonna Dow.

CHARACTERS

KEN: Kenneth Tynan. Smoker. 53. Oxonian, occasional stutter. Dandified in dress, but gone a bit to seed. He holds his cigarettes between his ring and middle finger.

LULU: Ken's fantasy, based on the character Lulu as portrayed by Louise Brooks in G.W. Pabst's 1928 silent film Pandora's Box. Smoker. Black bobbed hair. The quintessential flapper.

LOUISE: Louise Brooks. Smoker. 71. Long grey hair, pulled back into pony tail, no bangs, no makeup. Long nightgown with cheap bed jacket and orthopaedic slippers. Walks with a four-pronged medical cane.

NB: All three actors must be completely comfortable with continuous cigarette smoking. Tobacco cigarettes are preferred.

SETTING

The stage is divided into three areas. A black projection screen hangs above for slide and film projections.

Upstage right is Louise's room. A bed, a nightstand with telephone, and later, a kitchen chair. No real doors or windows.

Upstage left, an elevated area where Lulu makes her appearances, with steps leading downstage.

Downstage left, a large ottoman draped in black satin, and a standing art deco ashtray. This is Ken's area, where he is often joined by Lulu.

FILM CLIPS

The videos were edited to remove the titles and shots that involved additional characters. Other clips have been edited for time. Please contact the playwright for details.

AUTHOR'S NOTE

Emphysema is a work of fiction based on the actual meeting of Kenneth Tynan and Louise Brooks in 1978, and Tynan's subsequent *New Yorker Magazine* profile, "The Girl in the Black Helmet," published in 1979. The author acknowledges indebtedness to the writings of both Brooks and Tynan, and to numerous other biographical sources.

In blackout, a cigarette is lit. Spot up slowly on KEN, *standing. He takes a drag and exhales, watching the smoke in the stage light. He has a stutter which he uses to great effect.*

KEN: There is no piece of stage business more brilliant than this. Nothing more personal. Nothing more sexual. There is nothing more elegant, more indifferent, nothing that draws the eyes to the beautiful hand, the sensual mouth, the hypnotic gaze, the breath made manifest.

The lifting to one's lips, the element of fire, the suck, the burn, the glowing ember, the excruciating eternity before the pleasure, the climax, the sigh, the ashes.

Takes another drag to illustrate.

It is a kiss blown off the edge of the stage and out into the dark that says, fuck you, darlings. I know you're out there. But you are nothing to me. Look at you, watching me. At this moment, I am your entire world.

And another, taking his time.

I'm creating the atmosphere.

And another.

I'm making you wait for me.

How can you help but fall in love with the curl of smoke above my head? Soon it will reach out to you, a tender and illicit lover. Is it secretly touching you now? Is it stroking your face, your eyes, caressing the rim of your nostril? The wraith that haunts you now has been deep inside my body, inside my lungs. It was, for one breath, the air I breathed. My inspiration.

Inspire... *(He inhales.)*

Expire. *(He exhales.)*

Salvador Dali told me that his ideal erotic experience would involve two people whose sexual responses were so acute that they could stand at opposite ends of a huge baronial hall, dressed in shrouds with only slits for the eyes, and by looking at each other in a certain way achieve orgasm.

I suppose if one could get an actress to look at an audience like that, that would be it. But we still have this moment together, darlings, where I can touch you without touching you.

TITLE SLIDES:
Projected on wall behind playing area. Their typestyle, borders, and white writing on black background suggest silent film titles.

TITLE SLIDE: EMPHYSEMA

TITLE SLIDE: WITH

TITLE SLIDE: LOUISE BROOKS

TITLE SLIDE: AND

TITLE SLIDE: KENNETH TYNAN

Lights change to LOUISE *in bed, smoking and surrounded by books and papers. She is writing rapidly and crossing things out. Something blocks her train of thought and she picks up the phone on her bedside table and dials.*

VOICE: Rochester Public Library. *(Pause.)* Hello?

LOUISE: Is this the Rochester Public Library?

VOICE: Yes it is, ma'am.

LOUISE: I was wondering if you could tell me how one spells "catastrophe."

VOICE: Catastrophe. C, A, T, A, S, T, R, O, P, H, E. *(Pause.)* Ma'am? Did you get that? Hello?

LOUISE: *(Writing it down.)* Yes. Thank you, darling. *(She continues to write as she hangs up the phone. She picks up the phone again and dials.)*

VOICE: Rochester Public Library.

LOUISE: How do you spell "catastrophe" again?

VOICE: Is this Miss Brooks?

LOUISE: Fuck off. *(She hangs up and goes back to writing. Phone rings.)*

LOUISE: Oh, what! What! What! *(Picks up the phone.)* Who's this?

VOICE: This is the Rochester Public Library, Miss Brooks.

LOUISE: How did you get my number?

VOICE: Miss Brooks, it has come to our attention that books taken out in your name have been returned to the library in a condition that we consider unacceptable.

LOUISE: Will you get on with it? I'm a sick old woman and you're wasting the last few precious moments of my life.

VOICE: Miss Brooks, we have to ask you to stop making corrections in the film history books you borrow.

LOUISE: Are you calling me a vandal?

VOICE: We ask that you respect the books we send you if you wish to retain your borrowing privileges.

LOUISE: Privilege? To read that garbage?

VOICE: Miss Brooks, I need to inform you that this is a circulating library. The books must circulate. But when you write notes and corrections in the margins of our film history books, and people recognise the marginalia as yours, they steal the books.

LOUISE: Well, maybe they recognise the truth.

VOICE: Miss Brooks, these thieves are not film historians. Our film section has been decimated.

LOUISE: Decimated. Decimated?

VOICE: Yes. It means…

LOUISE: You idiot, of course I know what decimated means. Do you know what it means?

VOICE: Well, yes.

LOUISE: I don't think you do, darling.

VOICE: Miss Brooks…

LOUISE: It means to select every tenth man for punishment. And that is something that I know something about, you pretentious little shit.

VOICE: I'm sure you've had a fascinating life, Miss Brooks. I read Kenneth Tynan's profile of you in *The New Yorker*.

LOUISE: So I guess you think you know me pretty well. I guess you think you know me well enough to tell me how to behave.

VOICE: It was a wonderful tribute to you, Miss Brooks. I thought about it when I read his obituary last month.

           LOUISE is silent.

VOICE: Are you still there, Miss Brooks?

LOUISE: Bastard.

VOICE: I'm sorry?

LOUISE: What did it say about him?

VOICE: The obituary? He had emphysema. He was fifty-three. He said an indecent word on live television.

LOUISE: Anything else?

VOICE: Well, he was a drama critic. And that sex musical, *Oh! Calcutta!*, that was his.

LOUISE: That's it?

VOICE: I can look it up for you and send you a copy.

           LOUISE hangs up. Pause. She picks up the phone again and dials.

VOICE: Rochest...

LOUISE: How do you spell decimated?

VOICE: Miss Brooks, I have to ask you to stop calling every...

LOUISE: Spell it!

VOICE: D, E, C, I, M, A, T, E, D.

LOUISE: Thanks, darling. *(She hangs up. Lights fade.)*

FILM:
Opening credits of *Pandora's Box,* leading into
LULU's entrance.

Lights come up slowly on KEN, watching the film.

KEN: None of this would have happened if I'd not noticed in
my *TV Guide* that at 1:00 p.m. on a sunny afternoon I
could view a film on which my fantasies had fed since I
first saw it, a quarter of a century before.

He watches the film.

I wondered how many of my Santa Monican
neighbours would be lured away from a pool-side
brunch to watch a silent picture, shot in Berlin in 1928.
The story of an artless young hedonist who, meaning no
harm, rewards herself and her lovers with the prize of
violent death. Lulu.

*KEN turns back to the film and watches silently for a
moment as the film Lulu pours the meter man a drink.*

I think of the scene in *Citizen Kane,* when Bernstein tells
the story of how, in his youth, he saw the girl in the
white dress for an instant, from a distance, and not a
month goes by that he doesn't think of that girl.

*LULU enters upstage. She is dressed like the screen Lulu,
a bottle tucked under her arm.*

KEN: Look at her. Look at her.

KEN continues to watch the screen.

KEN: She wears beaded dresses in the afternoon, sips cocktails in the Library Bar where only men go, where the light is always Manhattan in the first week of November, 4:30 p.m. In my childhood dream of my life in the adult world, she is my heroine. Aristocratic, sophisticated, cosmopolitan. And so modern.

LULU sits and parts her robe slightly, extending her leg to straighten a black stocking.

LULU: Darling.

KEN: I own this girl. *(Still watching the film.)* She is bound to every fantasy, to every erotic notion, to the very idea of sex, bound hand and foot to the bedpost with a silk stocking.

LULU: Darling?

KEN: Darling.

LULU: Come on, darling. *(He hesitates.)* Come on. Have a drink, darling?

KEN: Of course. Was someone here? Before me?

LULU: *(Pouring his drink and handing him a glass.)* Just the man who reads the meter. Bottoms up, darling.

KEN: Who?

LULU: The delivery boy.

KEN: And?

LULU: The milkman, the cameraman, the stuntman…

KEN: Rapacious harlot.

LULU: Oh, darling, I'm a tramp, not a whore.

KEN: You have been a very naughty little girl, Lulu. You'll
        have to be punished.

LULU: No! No!

KEN: A wicked little vixen.

LULU: NO!

KEN: Take that off.

LULU: I won't! *(She drops her robe. Underneath, she is wearing
        complicated erotic underwear, garters etc.)*

KEN: Down.

LULU: I won't! I won't! *(She throws herself down and he spanks her
        with his glove while she shrieks.)* No! Help! Have mercy on
        me! Pity me! You...you...

                        FILM:
                Pandora's Box: Theatre scene between Lulu
                and Schön, in the props room. Actors sync up
                with film action for rest of scene. Lulu pounds
                the pillow with her fist, shakes her head from
                side to side, and kicks her legs in a very
                erotically charged tantrum.

KEN: Oh, but I do, you despicable hoyden. *(He sits next to her,
        at same time as Schön in film, shaking his head. He begins to
        laugh at her display. She sees this and becomes angry, sits up
        and pounds him with her fists. They grapple, and kiss. LULU
        looks up and smiles mischievously.)*

KEN: *(To audience.)* You see...

                *LULU searches though his pockets for a cigarette like a
                child looking for candy. When she finds his cigarette case
                she opens it and takes a cigarette greedily.*

LULU: Do you have a light, darling?

KEN: *(Lighting her cigarette.)...*she is a ruinous cobra, but she fascinates.

LULU: Thanks, darling. *(LULU exits.)*

           KEN lights his own cigarette and sits alone for a moment.

KEN: Dear Miss Brooks.

           LOUISE enters. She sits on the bed and reads a letter as KEN speaks.

KEN: Dear Miss Brooks. You probably don't know me, but I am an English author and drama critic, and former literary manager of the National Theatre of Great Britain. Last year I moved to the states to work for *The New Yorker,* and write a series of articles about people whom I admire. I recently saw *Pandora's Box* for a third time and my admiration for you was instantly rekindled.

           LULU is revealed in the background, scantily clad as before. Her arms are over her head. Her wrists and mouth are bound with wide black patent leather straps.

KEN: I am interested in meeting you at your home in Rochester to discuss your life and films for a Profile. *(LULU begins to fidget.)* When I remarked to my editor that I had an interest in you...

LULU: *(From behind her gag.)* Darling?

KEN: Hmm?

LULU: *(Pulls down her gag.)* How much longer?

KEN: In a moment.

           LULU pulls up her gag again.

I was pleasantly surprised when he told me that you were still living. Living in New York, and that you had published a number of brilliant articles on your film experiences and the people you worked with in Hollywood and Berlin.

I would like to meet with you at your home in Rochester in late April. If we could spend two or three sessions talking about your fascinating life, I would be very…

LULU whines for attention.

KEN: Shut up a moment, will you darling? I do so look forward to the opportunity of meeting you. Yours sincerely. Kenneth Tynan.

To audience.

You'll excuse us.

To LULU.

You bad thing!

Lights change to LOUISE, in bed, who reads over the letter she has written in reply.

LOUISE: Dear Mr Tynan. I am writing this fast and mailing it fast so I won't be able to take it back. I usually mark unfamiliar correspondence "deceased." So sorry to disappoint you, but I have none of the qualities you've assigned to her flickering self up there on the screen. And as for a lengthy *New Yorker* profile, I don't know if there's a person on this earth that I couldn't sum up in a thousand words. So the answer is no.

LOUISE is distracted by the sound of a garbage truck pulling up outside

LOUISE: Regards, Louise Brooks. P.S. As for knowing who you are, Mr Tynan. I know. And I believe you are a very naughty boy. *(A few loud crashes and honks interrupt her.)* What the hell is going on out there? *(Crossing to her window.)* What the hell is going on? What are you doing? Is that necessary? Don't you have any respect for a person's right to a little peace? *(A metal trash can and lid are thrown and roll down the street.)* Pick that up! You pick that up! Don't you dare leave, you bastard! *(Truck drives away.)* You pick that up! Bastard. *(She turns back to her letter and adds a further postscript.)*

LOUISE: P.P.S. If you must come, bring a gun.

Lights change.

PHOTO SLIDE:
Portrait of a young Louise with long strand of pearls.

KEN appears in light, rehearsing for their meeting.

TITLE SLIDE:
REHEARSAL

KEN: Darling! Darling. Oh, hello, darling. Louise. Darling Louise. Miss Brooks. Darling.

Lights up on LULU, posing as in the photograph, with a single floor-length strand of pearls looped over her outstretched hand.

LULU: Darling!

KEN: Darling, you look darling, darling.

LULU: Darling, you are a darling to say so.

KEN: Drink, darling?

LULU: Of course, darling. *(She produces glasses and a bottle, and he pours.)* Oh darling, I have waited all my life for this moment.

KEN: I suppose you have. *(He raises his glass.)* To you.

LULU: To you.

KEN: Oh, darling, oh *one*, let us often, that is to say, always, read the same books.

LULU: Oh, daaaaaaarling.

KEN: We shall have brilliant conversation. Here is a list for you of essential reading.

LULU: *Communist Manifesto, The Necessity of Art, Tynan on Tynan.*

KEN: I will bring out everything that is possible in you. But you will never come to me with your troubles.

LULU: Never, darling. I understand completely.

KEN: I should tell you that I have unusual sexual tastes.

LULU: Darling?

KEN: I like to spank girls. Are you terribly shocked?

LULU: Why no, darling.

KEN: Then you must worship me plainly. You must dress as I tell you. I shall take lovely photographs of you looking terrifically European.

LULU: I can't allow that.

KEN: Whyever not, darling?

LULU: Because when you take my picture you steal my soul, darling.

KEN: Then we must be seen together always. Laughing, fighting.

LULU: Let there always be something going on between us.

KEN: Suspicion, jealousy, intrigue, sudden meetings.

LULU: Let us pretend not to care.

KEN: Let us lose touch with each other for months.

LULU: Years! Let us forget each other completely.

KEN: When we forget each other, we shall cease to exist.

LULU: Forget me quickly, darling, I beg you.

KEN: I can't, darling. There's a curse on you. Now that I've seen you I cannot ever undo seeing you. Ever since I first looked upon your wonderful and incomparable beauty, I have dared to love you wildly, passionately, devotedly, hopelessly.

LULU: Oh, darling.

KEN: I hope I shall not offend you if I state quite frankly and openly that you seem to me to be in every way the visible personification of absolute perfection.

LULU: I think your frankness does you great credit, Earnest. If you will allow me, I will copy your remarks into my diary.

KEN: Oh, stop.

LULU: What, darling?

KEN: Stop, stop.

LULU: Why?

KEN: This is *The Importance of Being Earnest*. We're doing *The Importance of Being Earnest*.

LULU: Oh. *(Pause.)* Do you want to tie me up, then?

KEN: Maybe later.

          Lights change.

TITLE SLIDE:
DOROTHY

          LOUISE is lying in bed, smoking, several books, articles, research lying around her. She is reading a copy of Tynan's Curtains. LOUISE flips over the book to study KEN's picture. A knock at the door.

LOUISE: I don't want any! *(Eventually a knock.)*

LOUISE: *(Shouting.)* I don't want any, I said.

KEN: *(Offstage, stammering.)* It's me. It's Ken. Miss Brooks. I know I'm a bit early. Your neighbour let me up. I could come back later.

LOUISE: Just a minute. Just a minute. Just a minute, I'll be right there.

          KEN is dressed for outdoors in a long black coat, scarf, gloves. Bottle of wine, leather bag.

KEN: Ah, *(Coughing fit.)* hello. It's me.

LOUISE: *(Letting him in.)* You're too early.

KEN: *(Trying to catch his breath.)* I'm very sorry. *(Coughs.)* Excuse me. I hope It's not too inconvenient. If you're busy I can come back...

LOUISE: So you're the illustrious Kenneth Tynan, hmm?

KEN: Yes.

LOUISE: You're different than I imagined.

KEN: Oh?

LOUISE: I've been reading your books.

KEN: Oh, I see.

LOUISE: You're different than I thought. In real life, you don't look so...

KEN: Young?

LOUISE: Intelligent. You look too...hmmm, wicked. Like a satyr.

KEN: How marvellous.

LOUISE: I never imagined that you'd have a— *(She waves vaguely at her lips.)*

KEN: Oh, the, uh, stammer. You hardly notice it when I write.

LOUISE: I hope I didn't offend you.

KEN: No, of course not.

LOUISE: I think it's gorgeous.

KEN: It rarely bothers me these days. When I'm upset or excited. Nervous.

LOUISE: Are you nervous now?

KEN: *(Laughs.)* Yes, I'm very nervous.

LOUISE: Good. Well, come in, this place is a dump.

KEN: Not at all.

LOUISE: I bet I'm not quite what you had in mind.

KEN: Oh, no, really, yes.

LOUISE: Liar.

KEN: Yes. Well, I must say this is a very great pleasure... I
          brought you a bottle...'59 Burgundy. Supposed to be a
          very good year.

LOUISE: I wouldn't know. I was drunk that year.

KEN: Oh. *(Alarmed.)* Do you not...then you don't...?

LOUISE: What the hell. It's a special occasion. It's a party
          compared with the rest of my life.

KEN: Ha.

                    Pause.

LOUISE: Well.

KEN: Yes?

LOUISE: Are you waiting for the sun to cross over the yardarm?

KEN: Oh, pah. Shall I? I'll look after this, shall I?

LOUISE: Give it to me. I'll do it. *(As she exits, making circles in the
          air with her finger.)* Where's your goddamn thingy? The
          thingy is over there. *(Makes plugging-in gesture.)*

KEN: Tape recorder? No, I don't have one.

                    *LOUISE enters with open bottle and plastic tumblers. He
                    pours, swirls his wine in the tumbler, holds it up to the
                    light...*

LOUISE: Bottoms up.

KEN: I suppose we should get started.

LOUISE: I'm desperately tired.

KEN: I could come back tomorrow.

LOUISE: Might as well get it over with now that you're here.

> *LOUISE starts to get into bed. She is having some trouble and KEN doesn't know if he should help.*

KEN: Here, let me...

LOUISE: *(Pointing to the tray table.)* Just get that out of the way.

KEN: Here okay?

LOUISE: Thanks, sweetie. *(She picks up the book.)* Sign it. Not for me. For Marge. She's my upstairs neighbour. I'd be dead if it weren't for her. Brings me three meals a day, doesn't ask for a dime. She's a darling and I'm just wicked to her, just wicked. I can't help it. She's one of those caring, concerned types that you want to, oh, kick.

KEN: Is she interested in the theatre?

LOUISE: No. She's interested in famous people.

KEN: I see.

LOUISE: She's never heard of you.

KEN: Well, that's fine.

LOUISE: I didn't tell her about your *Oh! Calcutta!*, or that you're the man who said "fuck" on live TV.

KEN: Yes. My epitaph. *(As he hands the book to her, his attention is caught by LOUISE's shoes. She notices KEN staring at them.)*

LOUISE: Is there a problem with my shoes?

KEN: I'm sorry.

LOUISE: Space shoes.

KEN: I'm sure they're very comfortable, darling.

LOUISE: *(Laughing.)* Look at you. You should just see yourself. You just don't know what to think, do you, mister *enfant terrible?*

KEN: I haven't been that for thirty years. *(He offers her a cigarette and she takes it.)*

LOUISE: Adult *ordinare.* I'm just giving you a hard time. Have a light, darling?

KEN: Of course.

LOUISE: So. What do you want?

KEN: I'm interested in your life, your work. Your beginnings as a dancer, your time on Broadway with Ziegfield Follies, your Hollywood films, your work with Pabst in Berlin. Why you walked away from films at the height of your career.

LOUISE: Why do you think?

KEN: That's what I'm here to find out.

LOUISE: You tell me.

KEN: I think you had integrity.

LOUISE: Maybe I was just bored.

KEN: I've read your magazine pieces about film acting, and the corruption of the Hollywood system—I think they're fabulous.

LOUISE: You're bullshitting me, darling.

KEN: I'm not! You're a very talented writer.

LOUISE: You slay me. *(Smiling.)* You really want to sit here for three days and talk to a mean old bag about her utterly, utterly, miserable life? I know what you really want.

KEN: What do I want?

LOUISE: You want her.

> *LULU pops up over the headboard of the bed. She is wearing a corset and transparent striped Victorian bloomers. She sits on the headboard, her ankles crossed, inches away from LOUISE.*

KEN: I don't know what you're talking about.

LOUISE: You do. She might live in your fantasy world, sweetheart, but believe me, you don't live in hers.

KEN: Nonsense, darling.

LOUISE: I've been trying to kill her off for fifty years, and everyone wants to bring her back to life.

KEN: Darling, you have to forgive people admiring you. They can't help it.

LOUISE: But they don't exist to me.

KEN: But you exist to them. The entire western world has a collective memory of your face—the face you see in your mind when you think of the twenties. You embody a time and place in history.

LOUISE: Yeah? Well, that's not my problem.

KEN: Some people wouldn't think of that as a problem

LOUISE: You, maybe.

KEN: Darling, I think it's an honour. You're an icon.

LOUISE: An icon.

KEN: Yes!

LOUISE: Imagine this. At this moment, somewhere in the world, someone you've never met, is obsessed with you. They're thinking about you right now. They're looking at a grimy old photograph of you that they ripped out of a library book and keep folded up at the bottom of the sock drawer. Their whole life revolves around meeting you. They think, if only—if only the two of you could meet, you would suddenly know, somehow, that this was the person that the cosmos had created to make you complete. That kind of crap. Now, would you feel good about that? Would you feel safe?

KEN: But surely, darling, that is what it means to be a celebrity.

           LULU crawls off the bed to kneel at KEN's feet. She rubs up against his leg like a cat.

LOUISE: No thanks, darling. I don't want to be a celebrity. Somebody that other people project their sick and unwholesome fantasies on? She's a light on the screen for chrissake! Emulsion in a few cans of disintegrating film. She doesn't exist!

KEN: But you do.

LOUISE: Even if she was real, she's dead. I killed her. I drank, smoked, and fucked her into oblivion, pardon my french. But you know what really stuck the knife in her, darling? I got old.

KEN: Now...

LOUISE: I got old. Face it, this face is fifty years older than the one
            you had in mind when you were outside my door. True
            or False.

KEN: Let's not talk about her any more. Let's talk about you

            LULU looks up at KEN, hurt, then exits.

KEN: You were born in Kansas, 1906.

LOUISE: Yeah. Like Dorothy.

KEN: Like Dorothy. *(Pause.)* A little girl plucked from the
            cornfields who, at the end of her trip to a magical world,
            finds that happiness was in her own backyard.

LOUISE: Not quite.

KEN: No?

LOUISE: I was thinking of a Dorothy who runs away from home
            at fourteen and lands in a goddamn magical world full of
            freaks who want to rob her. She is unable to worship
            those mighty men of power whom she does not admire.
            And at the end of her usefulness to the cowards, the
            fools, and the heartless bastards, she limps into obscurity
            never to venture forth again.

KEN: I see.

LOUISE: Yes, I love that movie. Oh, you're disappointed.

KEN: I'm not disappointed.

LOUISE: You are disappointed. I should have said I like some
            deep movie.

KEN: And now, "There's no place like home?"

LOUISE: Oh, please. That line nearly ruined it for me.

KEN: Let's talk about—your daily life.

LOUISE: Who'd want to know about that? I spend 80% of my time in bed.

KEN: So do I.

Lights change as title slide comes up.

TITLE SLIDE:
ROSEBUD

KEN sitting, legs crossed, notebook on his knee. He has a drink and a cigarette in one hand, pen in the other. LULU is revealed upstage. Lights up on LULU. She is wearing a transparent version of Dorothy's gingham dress.

LULU: Whatcha doin'?

KEN: Work.

LULU: Play with me.

KEN: Not tonight, darling. I'm busy.

LULU: Too busy for me?

KEN: Too tired.

LULU: Tired of me?

KEN: Just tired.

LULU: Then it must be time for bed. *(Moving in to him.)* I know what you need. You need a little pick-me-up. Hmm? Then you'll feel more like your old self. *(Whispering in his ear.)* More like your old, old self.

KEN: Piss off.

LULU: Don't you love me any more? That's it. You don't love
          me anymore. You dislove me.

KEN: It's not that. Good heavens, what are you wearing?

LULU: Oh, no darling! You don't mean to say…you…you…
          respect me? *(Swooning and shielding her eyes from the light.)*
          Ohhhhhh. Ohhhhhh. I'm feeling faint! *(As if she can see
          through her hand.)* Look! I'm disappearing! I'm vanishing!
          Look at me! Look! Look! I'm melting! *(She melts, and
          pounds the floor when he doesn't look up.)* Look at me.
          Look! I'm dissolving! *(Her voice becomes faint, à la
          Camille.)* Goodbye, darling! I'm fading away! *(A couple of
          faint tubercular coughs.)* Goodbye…*(Croaks hoarsely.)*
          Rosebud… *(She dies.)*

                    KEN looks up.

KEN: Still with us?

LULU: *(Sitting up.)* I'm better now. *(She flips through one of his
          notebooks.)* What's this?

KEN: Notes for the profile. Snatches of conversation.

LULU: And vice versa!

KEN: This profile could get us back on track. It could change
          everything.

LULU: How you feel about me?

KEN: Never, darling.

LULU: We'll see.

                    *KEN returns to his work. LULU slithers over but he
                    ignores her. She slithers into a position to be able to read*

over his shoulder. When KEN realises what she is doing, he covers the page with his hand.

KEN: Stop it! You make me hate you when you do that.

LULU climbs over his shoulder, on top of his book and onto his lap, looking up at him. After an exasperated pause, KEN gives in and kisses her.

KEN: Don't force me to kill you in self defence, darling.

LULU: It's the only way you'll get rid of me.

Lights fade on KEN.

TITLE SLIDE:
FOLLIES

KEN and LOUISE are looking at photos and clippings from a box, drinking and smoking.

LOUISE: Look. At. Her.

KEN: An angel whore.

LOUISE: Not good enough to be an angel, too dumb to be a whore. I mean, look where I'm spending my golden years. I was never any good at spoiling men.

KEN: Where is this?

LOUISE: Don't you know? That's Joe Zelli's in Paris, darling. I'm stewed in this one, all right. Oh, and look at that dress! Half naked in the afternoon!

KEN: I've never seen a photo with so much of the twenties in it. Who are all these gentlemen? Mobsters?

LOUISE: Ha, I don't know—oh, no, wait. I went to bed with him. And him. He gave me a silver fox stole and I let him take me to a tea dance just once. Oh, what a heartless racket. This one gave me a hundred bucks for the powder room.

KEN: I say. *(Picking up another photo.)*

LOUISE: He was a bastard. *(Looking at the next photo.)* My God! Is she ever sexy. Look at those gams!

KEN: Lyric.

LOUISE: They aren't that great.

KEN: The first time I saw you was when I was at Oxford in the forties, in a old *Photoplay* magazine, from '26. You were in bed, just like this, when they photographed you. The reporter described you as "So very Manhattan. Very young. Exquisitely hard-boiled... Her legs are lyric."

LOUISE: Yeah, yeah. I never read anything written about me that didn't make me puke.

KEN: If she doesn't have it, I don't know what it is.

LOUISE: Who does? That's why they called it It.

KEN: The ability to project one's entire personality, one's soul, with a minimum of visible effort. High definition performance. That's why I love you, darling.

LOUISE: Shut up.

KEN: The jazz baby sophisticate.

LOUISE: You slay me, you just slay me!

KEN: What? What did I say?

LOUISE: I didn't want that kind of life!

KEN: Well, then?

LOUISE: What?

KEN: What kind of life did you want?

LOUISE: Well, your life. I wanted to read books, and write, and be with brilliant people.

KEN: Not exactly the American Dream.

LOUISE: You got that right. Oh, everyone thought I was such a snob, reading Proust between takes instead of the *Police Gazette*. They hated me and my superior attitude!

KEN: Must have been hair-raising to see the most beautiful woman of the 20th Century turning the pages of Faust.

LOUISE: Oh, yeah. You know, Mr. Pabst moved to Hollywood from Berlin in the thirties to make a movie of Faust with me as Helen and Garbo as Gretchen!

KEN: Fantastic! What happened?

LOUISE: Hollywood wouldn't give him the money to do it, and certainly not with *moi*, so he went back to Germany to make films for the Nazis.

KEN: What a waste.

LOUISE: All I made after that was a couple of crap westerns. It was in the cards for us flappers anyway. Sex symbols were changing. When Garbo arrived, oh! we were in despair!

KEN: She never did anything for me, darling.

LOUISE: Darling, Garbo was never meant for you, she was meant for women.

KEN: She did have the most thrilling walk. But she was much too perfect to be really...

LOUISE: Yeah. Real ice goddess. She made a pass at me once, at a party. My God, she was a terrific star. She was really gorgeous, really knew what she was doing. Know her?

KEN: Not really.

LOUISE: No. Who did? *(She unfolds a newspaper clipping.)*

KEN: Not much on there, darling.

LOUISE: That's in Ziegfield Follies.

KEN: How did the cornfields produce that?

LOUISE: I do not know.

KEN: That's what the American male thinks is beautiful. Shiny things moving with mechanical precision.

LOUISE: You got that right.

KEN: There's something so sublime about the showgirl.

LOUISE: It was too, too divine. I was just nineteen in 1925. Me and Charlie swinging into the Lido, furs dripping off my shoulders. And I tell you, I was magnificent then. I had this lethal gold lace dress, terribly itchy but divine, and the dance floor cleared when we did the tango.

KEN: Charlie?

LOUISE: Oh it was marvellous. For two months, while he was opening *The Gold Rush,* two perfect summer months. It was like a fairy tale. And he was like—an enchanted prince.

KEN: Chaplin?

LOUISE: You should have seen him then. He was just so clean, you know? Just perfectly made, and small, and glowing all over like a pearl. He had this thing around him. Even when he was asleep.

KEN: My. My.

LOUISE: And you must remember that, at that time, he was the most famous man who ever lived. More famous than, say, oh...

KEN: Jesus Christ?

LOUISE: I heard there's this place on some island somewhere where they actually do worship him as a god, and I tell you, I would go there and be a disciple or whatever. He knew he was a genius who had created a great masterpiece—that must be perfect happiness, don't you think? Hey?

KEN: Yes. What?

LOUISE: What do you think happens when you get what you really want—your heart's desire? When you achieve perfect happiness?

KEN: You become impotent.

LOUISE: You maybe. Not Charlie, that's for sure! Now, he was a very sophisticated lover. You can't imagine.

KEN: Can't I?

LOUISE: No.

KEN: You have to tell me about this, darling.

LOUISE: Oh, no no. So you can write me down and sell me to a dirty magazine for money? The unbelievable sexcapades of the wild Louise Brooks.

KEN: Never. I wouldn't want to do that to you.

LOUISE: You will, though. *(Pause.)* You will want to.

KEN: You've led a life of sexual integrity.

LOUISE: Listen to you! Sexual integrity. I like that.

KEN: You wrote that sexuality is the only key there is to truly knowing a person.

LOUISE: It's the only way to explain why people do unexplainable things.

KEN: Like throwing away careers? Burning bridges?

LOUISE: Oh sure. I did what I wanted. What anyone would do.

KEN: Not everyone does what they want.

LOUISE: No? Stupid everyone, then. Fine, what anyone would do, given certain opportunities.

KEN: Looking like that.

LOUISE: Well, sure. Being that young.

KEN: And famous.

LOUISE: And not caring a good goddamn for anyone.

KEN: You must have left quite a trail of broken hearts.

LOUISE: Ha! To break someone's heart you have to care, and I say, who cares?

KEN: That's what Lulu says.

LOUISE: Oh, yes?

KEN: Yes. In the film, Alwa says "Do you love me, Lulu?" and she replies, "I? Never a soul!"

LOUISE: Well, fancy that!

KEN: So what happened?

LOUISE: What?

KEN: You and…the Little Tramp.

LOUISE: Well, summer ended. You know. And he sent me a nice
            big cheque. Be a sugarpie and loan me a cigarette, will
            you? I'm out.

            He does.

KEN: I have a confession. I once went to a costume party. I
            went. As you.

LOUISE: NO!

KEN: Oh, yes.

LOUISE: Did anyone know who you were supposed to be?

KEN: They asked, of course, and I told them "Baden Powell."

LOUISE: You lie!

KEN: I'd never lie to you darling. You'd find me out.

LOUISE: You're such a slut, darling.

KEN: I think we know who the slut is here.

LOUISE: You'd make one hell of an ugly woman.

KEN: Yes. But I really wanted to find out how it would feel.

LOUISE: To be a girl?

KEN: No, no, to be—oh, I don't know. *(Picking up another
            photo.)*

LOUISE: "The Brooks Bob." I was in all the salon windows, everybody wanted it—the haircut my mother gave me on a kitchen stool back in Witchita. I made twenty-four films and my hairstyle is the one thing about me that will endure. Pathetic, isn't it?

KEN: You're were terribly "in" in the 60's.

LOUISE: I'll come around again, no doubt. It's a comfort, really. No one knows who the hell I am, but I come back into vogue every fifteen years.

KEN: You're too much, darling.

LOUISE: What about you? What will you endure as? "The man who said 'fuck' on TV?"

          Pause.

LOUISE: I was joking!

KEN: It's no joke.

LOUISE: Listen, you're a real success. You've written books. People care about what you think. Hell, you tell people what to think.

KEN: It's not the same as creating something new. It comes easily to some people. People who can walk in front of a camera, for instance, and create a work of art.

LOUISE: I never asked for it.

KEN: And I'll never achieve it.

LOUISE: Well, you can take it.

KEN: But I don't have what it takes to make it last.

LOUISE: "It."

KEN: That's it.

LOUISE: You know what Goethe said? He said that a man's life isn't important for what he leaves behind, but only if he acts and enjoys, and rouses others to action and enjoyment. Hey? That's just what you do.

KEN: Thank you.

LOUISE: To be a great person is the only work of art. *(She picks up another photo.)*

PHOTO SLIDE:
Teenaged Louise in a dancing costume, looking back over her shoulder.

KEN: What a wicked thing. A naughty altar boy.

LOUISE: That's when I was 15. Used to dance for Rotary.

KEN: God help us all.

         Lights change. KEN sits on ottoman, with a drink and a cigarette, watching LULU. LULU is lying on her back, legs in the air, reading a very thick book.

KEN: Come on, darling.

LULU: Did someone speak? Or was it the wind?

KEN: Come on.

LOUISE: Oh, it's you.

KEN: Yes, it's me. Come here.

LULU: You have time for me now, do you?

KEN: There's always time for you.

LULU: I thought you didn't want me anymore.

KEN: Of course I want...I need... *(KEN pulls her around to straddle him, kissing and caressing her. She does not look up from her book.)*

KEN: What's that?

LULU: This?

KEN: Yes. What are you reading?

LULU: *À la Recherche du Temps Perdu.*

KEN: Ha, ha. Very amusing.

LULU: "At the taste of the lime cordial-soaked madeleine, the past rose up in my mind like scenery at the theatre..."

KEN: *(Pushing her off.)* Oh no, now, look. Here's a magazine. *(Handing her one.)* Read that. Read *Vanity Fair.*

LULU: No.

KEN: Read a nice fashion magazine.

LULU: No, Proust! Proust!

KEN: It doesn't look right on you.

LULU: Why?

KEN: It looks...

LULU: Cheap?

KEN: Oh, never mind.

LULU: Read it to me.

KEN: I'm busy.

LULU: Come on. Come on and read it to me.

KEN: Where are we?

LULU: *(Pointing to her place.)* Here.

KEN: "The time which we have at our disposal each day is elastic. Passions expand it, those we inspire contract it, and habit fills up the remains."

         LULU crosses her legs and rubs them together.

KEN: Don't do that, darling. You'll set yourself alight.

TITLE SLIDE:
OCCUPATIONAL HAZARDS

FILM:
Schön's first entrance, to tell Lulu he is getting married.

         Ken is alone. He lights a cigarette. His breathing is slightly, but noticeably, laboured.

KEN: I spent my life taking people's breath away. Now it appears I have to pay some kind of penalty.

         LULU enters, and she and KEN sync with the film until the end of his monologue.

My doctor made me a radioactive daiquiri and took x-rays of my lungs. Two spreading elms lit by moonlight, a few scattered leaves. He said it's time for oxygen therapy. But I just can't wear that scuba gear. It just doesn't go.

I've been advised to alter my lifestyle. But style is my life. Style before substance. Style before breath. By all means, Ken, continue to work, but indulge in pleasures other than smoking, drinking, amphetamines and sex.

Anyone?

EMPHYSEMA

I'm a Pandora's Box of glamorous little vices. If I relax, let down my guard, who knows what will fly out?

I live in my head. I have installed four stalwart locks on its door, to be opened by four sacred keys. Cigarettes. White wine. Dexymyl. And masturbation. When you live in your head, darlings, you need these little things to help you face the mess inside.

I need my keys to gain access, to work, but my weaknesses feed the disease. The emphysema...It's taken away the— I can't— I'm—

I've lost a key.

My intelligence stepped out of my body for a moment, for a breath of air, and the door clicked shut behind. I'm locked out. I'm desperate to get back in, I must, I'm helpless, pounding on the door, peering through the mail slot, all the bills, contracts, queries about work I promised, piling up on the floor. My gangster organs, conspiring against me for the damage I've done them, have broken in, ransacked the place, tipped over the furniture, scattered my files. They're huddled around the kitchen table, bickering over a pitiful cache of oxygen I had hidden in an old rubber boot at the back of the wardrobe.

I am breaking to pieces with anxiety, over working and not working. The fear of creating, of not being able to create. Fear of never being able to begin. Fear of becoming incoherent, of losing my mind, of losing myself, my one work of art, the one most impermanent thing. Of disappearing without a trace.

LULU: Come on. Come on, darling.

Lying on her back, LULU puts her arms around his neck to pull KEN down, or herself up, to be kissed. The kiss occurs on the screen, but KEN closes his eyes and shakes his head.

KEN: I can't even enjoy enjoying myself any more.

TITLE SLIDE:
VENUS FLYTRAP

PHOTO SLIDE:
LOUISE in *Pandora's Box,* in her mourning dress, lifting her veil.

LOUISE and KEN sitting together, looking at a photo.

KEN: Lulu.

LOUISE: Yeah.

They stare and smoke.

KEN: On trial for shooting her husband on her wedding night. That look. What are you thinking about?

LOUISE: What the hell do you think I was thinking about? I was thinking about what I was doing!

KEN: No, I know, darling, that's not what I mean. How can one look—it's like the rise and fall of civilization, darling. Right there. So innocent, so intelligent. So devastating.

LOUISE: I look like that because I didn't know how to act.

KEN: Well if you weren't acting, that's you up there.

LOUISE: You know, if you don't have the technique to protect yourself, you burn straight into that lens. That's why Mr. Pabst cast me.

KEN: Instead of a German actress.

LOUISE: He looked all over the world for somebody to play Lulu. But the German actresses were too, oh, whorish. Then he saw me in some pointless little movie; I was playing a bathing beauty, or somebody's bad little sister, whatever, and he knew that he'd found his Lulu.

KEN: They say Pabst's greatest artistic achievement was casting you and letting you make the film for him.

LOUISE: Who says that?

KEN: Film historians.

LOUISE: That is bullshit.

KEN: Fine. I say that. Nothing else he did came close to the two films he made with you. *Pandora's Box* is a masterpiece because of you, whether or not you knew what you were doing.

LOUISE: You don't understand anything. He was a genius. And I was a great disappointment to him. I refused to be a serious actress. I was sleeping with the actor who played Jack the Ripper at the time, and to keep us from going to the nightclubs, Mr. Pabst would lock me in my room at night.

KEN: Well, I gather Berlin in '29 was a hothouse of sex, fabulous parties, artist's balls—

LOUISE: The works! You'd have loved it, darling, so debauched, just divine! I was staying at the Eden Hotel!

KEN: It would have been irresponsible to be responsible.

LOUISE: The first night he locked me up—what a tantrum I threw! I howled like the poor caged beasts in the zoo across the street. But the next night, it was straight out the window, still drunk on horrid German champagne when I showed up for work in the morning. But I couldn't fool Mr. Pabst . And for the first time I started to feel—what?

KEN: Guilt.

LOUISE: Like I deserved to be punished. At first I thought it might be that I was in love.

KEN: With Jack the Ripper.

LOUISE: No, with Mr. Pabst. That was my finest performance, the night I slept with him. He wasn't the same with me after that. He told me to clean up my act, that I'd end up just like Lulu, that I deserved whatever I got, but you know, I didn't listen. It scared the hell out of me, but I didn't listen.

KEN: You were Lulu to him, the lost girl. He wanted to save you.

LOUISE: Someone's always trying to save me. Makes them feel better about themselves.

KEN: Does it?

LOUISE: Doesn't it? Mr. Pabst really knew how to get—inside me. He guided my actions, my thoughts, with his voice while the camera was rolling. Like a conscience. It was, oh, how can I describe…very…

KEN: Intimate.

LOUISE: Oh, yes.

KEN: You reinvented film acting. Complete simplicity.

LOUISE: I was just supposed to stand in front of the camera and have sex with everyone and they'd all drop like flies.

KEN: The Venus Flytrap.

LOUISE: Here was I, so holy, so fed up with Hollywood, in a
            country where I couldn't speak a word, and so happy. I
            trusted him completely. Mr. Pabst's voice was always
            there inside my head.

KEN: Telling you what to do.

LOUISE: No, making me feel. Like this.

                              FILM:
              Wedding night scene of *Pandora's Box*. Schön
              offers Lulu a gun to kill herself "to save them
              both" but she accidentally shoots and kills
              him.

LOUISE: *(As film Lulu looks at herself in the mirror and removes her
            pearls.)* Look at you. You're radiant. You make the
            pearls jealous that circle your neck. Thank them, thank
            them, before you put them to sleep. Don't let them feel
            sad that they are not you.

                    *As she puts the pearls down Schön appears behind Lulu
                    in the mirror.*

            At last, alone, with him, this moment, this night. Why
            does he look at you that way? You've done nothing.
            No, his eyes are filled with fear. How can he be afraid of
            you, a child?

                    Lulu backs away and Schön holds the gun out to her.

            Weren't you happy together a moment ago, drunk on
            champagne and dancing with your wedding guests?

                    Lulu and Schön struggle over the gun.

            Your dress, your lovely dress, your wedding dress, so
            cool and white, remember last night how you secretly

put it on, how it slid like a lover's hand over your skin and made you shiver?

> *In the struggle, the gun goes off and there is a puff of smoke as she shoots him and he falls slowly away from her.*

What have you done, Lulu? What have you done? You never did a thing you didn't want to do. And in this second everything has changed for you forever.

> *Schön touches her face, tries to kiss her, then falls at her feet, pulling down the shoulder of her dress.*

Look at him. What is that coming out of his mouth? *Das Blut. Das Blut*, Louise…

> *The film fades.*

LOUISE: Next morning I came to work drunk and he was furious. He said "Louissse, the story of Lulu is your story. You will meet the same end."

KEN: Did you?

LOUISE: Well, it's not like I read the script. It was a terrible flop. In America it just died, died on the vine. I swore I'd never see it. If I never knew what the end was, then I'd never meet it.

KEN: Lulu becomes a prostitute and a victim of Jack the Ripper.

LOUISE: Well, I knew I wound up with a knife in the vagina.

KEN: An unrepentant hedonist mustn't be rewarded.

LOUISE: But that was a reward for her. He was Jack the Ripper, for chrissake, he couldn't help but kill the thing he loved. And Lulu dies in the arms of her dream lover, a sexual maniac. What sweeter reward could there be for her?

KEN: Have you still not seen *Pandora's Box*?

LOUISE: In 1970, at a festival. Boy, was I drunk! I could really drink in those days.

KEN: What did you think of it?

LOUISE: Well, Pabst was wrong about me, for once. I didn't end up like Lulu. I saved myself. And here I am, fifty years later, still alive.

KEN: No seductive killers lurking in the shadows ?

LOUISE: That was the last time I was out.

KEN: That was the last time you went to a film?

LOUISE: No, I mean out.

KEN: The last time you were out?

LOUISE: Yeah.

KEN: That was eight years ago, darling.

LOUISE: Yeah.

KEN: Get dressed.

LOUISE: Why?

KEN: Get dressed. We're going out to dinner.

LOUISE: No, we are not.

KEN: Go get dressed. We'll go to the restaurant in my hotel. No, we'll go to that little place down the block.

LOUISE: No.

KEN: Look, darling. It will be fabulous. We'll celebrate. We'll drink champagne. We'll just have a wonderful, wonderful time that we'll never forget.

LOUISE: What is there to celebrate?

KEN: You. The Profile. And I have some wonderful news. I'll tell you all about it over dinner. Where's your coat?

LOUISE: Tell me now.

KEN: Oh, that'll spoil it. Let's wait till we're there.

LOUISE: I'm not going anywhere.

KEN: Fine. I've been talking to a few friends of mine, film people, but not Hollywood—New York people, people with integrity. You'd like them.

LOUISE: Well, good for you.

KEN: They're simply fascinated.

LOUISE: About what?

KEN: You. A film about your life. It's perfect. You'd have complete artistic control, I'd see to that. And with your permission, madame, I could supervise the script.

LOUISE: I don't believe this.

KEN: Look. I know I shouldn't say this, but I'm just mad about you, darling. I really think you are the most fascinating creature, and really—oh, so wicked—I just adore...

LOUISE: I see. You just want to make money off me. And when you're through with me you'll throw me right back into the gutter. *(She is finding it heard to breathe.)* No one's going to make a dime off of this old bag.

KEN: Look, forget it. If you don't want...

LOUISE: I'm the solution to all your problems, aren't I? Money? Writer's block? Or am I your newest sex toy? Are senior citizens the latest thing with all the really fashionable swingers?

KEN: I'm sorry.

LOUISE: You're sick!

KEN: Forget I said anything.

LOUISE: I trusted you. When I opened the door to you I thought, now, I could love this man. He could understand me. But you're just another opportunistic bastard. Get out.

KEN: Do you want some water? Have some water.

LOUISE: And now you've given me emphysema. Get out of here.

KEN: Should I call for help? I can get your neighbour.

LOUISE: Get out.

KEN: Please. Please be reasonable.

LOUISE: Get out.

KEN: Fine. *(He leaves without looking back.)* Good night.

Title Slide:
MONSTER

KEN is sitting alone, sulking. He has one hand on his waist, and in the other he holds a highball glass and a cigarette.

LULU is wrapped in a black silk sheet.

LULU: Darling?

Ken ignores her.

LULU: Come on, darling. Come on. *(No response.)* Darling? Darling? *(She shimmies in her shroud, coyly guarding what she has on underneath.)* I've got your favourite. *(Stamping her foot.)* Oh, come on, darling.

KEN: I have to work.

LULU: Have a look.

KEN: Would you be so kind as to leave me alone?

LULU: Have a look first. Have one little look. Then I'll go. I won't bother you again.

KEN: Just go. Just go.

LULU: Look first.

KEN: Excuse me. Can you tell me who is directing this fantasy sequence?

LULU: You are.

KEN: That's right, darling. So do go, now.

LULU: No.

KEN: *(Closing his eyes and covering his ears.)* Go.

LULU: Punish me!

KEN: No.

LULU: You'll want to. You'll want to when you see what I've got under here.

KEN: I can't. I'm not feeling well. I have to work. I have to work.

LULU drops the shroud. She is wearing LOUISE's bedjacket and holding a medical cane. She holds it jauntily at her hip, like Chaplin.

KEN: I can't ever, ever forgive you for that.

LULU looks at KEN long and sadly, then crosses, limping heavily on the cane, to the ottoman and produces a telephone. She sits, raises the receiver and dials a number as KEN watches.

The phone on LOUISE's bed rings. Lights up on her room. LOUISE picks up phone.

LOUISE: Hello? Hello?

LULU: Hello?

LOUISE: Who is this?

LULU: I'm calling on behalf of a mutual friend.

LOUISE: How did you get my number?

KEN wrestles the phone away from LULU, holding her back with one arm.

KEN: It's me. I'm sorry.

LOUISE: I thought you wouldn't want to talk to me again.

KEN: Of course I do.

LOUISE: I was—I was really just wicked to you. I didn't mean it. Come back.

KEN: Tomorrow.

LOUISE: Now. Come now.

KEN: Get some rest.

LOUISE: Mr. Pabst was right about me.

KEN: What do you mean?

LOUISE: I'm just like her. Like Lulu. I knew it.

KEN: Nonsense.

LOUISE: I cut myself off from everything for fifty years, just to prove him wrong.

KEN: And he was.

LOUISE: No, he was right. This is the end of my little movie. And here you are, my Jack.

>   LULU *hangs the phone up and strokes his hair as the lights fade.*

TITLE SLIDE:
PANDORA

>   LOUISE *in bed.* KEN *enters.*

KEN: Hello, darling.

LOUISE: Oh, hello there.

KEN: I brought you a present.

LOUISE: Oh. *Tynan Right and Left.* How thoughtful. I don't have anything to give you. Except a drink. Come on, have a drink, darling?

KEN: Of course, darling.

>   *She pours him a drink and hands him a glass.*

LOUISE: So. Let's just forget about my little outburst, shall we? We can still have a lovely evening. A lovely last evening together.

KEN: All right.

LOUISE: What do you want to do? Anything. Just pretend it never happened. Name it.

KEN: I don't mind.

Pause.

LOUISE: All right, then it's my turn to interview you. I've been blabbing on about myself for days and I don't really know a damn thing about you.

KEN: Fire away.

LOUISE: We'll start at the beginning. Where were you born?

KEN: Magdalen College, Oxford. 1945.

LOUISE: Let's see. That makes you…thirty-three?

KEN: Anything that happened before that is irrelevant.

LOUISE: Parents?

KEN: I'm a bastard, darling.

LOUISE: Genealogically or temperamentally?

KEN: I prefer to think that I'm artistic by temperament.

LOUISE: Don't worry. I always like the bastards best. I always had a passion for some kind of bastard. I didn't hurt your feelings?

KEN: No. I'm flattered.

LOUISE: Good. I'm improving. I was never any good at flattering men. Now, tell me about your family.

KEN: Wife, ex-wife. Three children. Mistress. Cat.

LOUISE: Oh, dear. Oh, no, you shouldn't have told me that. I shouldn't have asked. That ruins everything.

KEN: I'm sorry.

LOUISE: I hate cats.

KEN: Oh.

LOUISE: Marge says "Oh, Louise, you should get a cat! They're no bother and they're such nice company!" Oh, they're terrible. They never leave you alone. They lie on your books when you're reading, ruin your work... Ooooo touch me, pet me, I hate them! What's the matter with you?

KEN: Nothing. It's ...

LOUISE: What?

KEN: Oh, never mind.

LOUISE: I'm hardly in a position to judge other people's morals. You can't have it both ways.

KEN: Oh, darling, I can think of at least a hundred ways of having it.

LOUISE: So. Who are you going to "do" next? Now that you're finished with me.

KEN: I don't know. I have a lot of loose ends to tie up.

LOUISE: Before you go to Spain? (Pause.) You know, I've never been there. I bet it's wonderful. Tell me what it's like.

KEN: Oh, very arid.

LOUISE: Arid.

KEN: Lucid. Vivid. Sordid.

LOUISE: Torrid?

KEN: All the adjectives that end in "id".

LOUISE: It sounds sublime.

KEN: It is exactly that, like you. Sublime. Too beautiful to fear the consequences.

LOUISE: Sounds like our kind of place.

KEN: Come with me.

LOUISE: Me? To Spain?

KEN: Yes.

LOUISE: You're joking!

KEN: I'm not.

LOUISE: You're being cruel.

KEN: No, I mean it. Come to Spain. I rent a villa. There's plenty of room.

LOUISE: What on earth would I do in Spain?

KEN: Whatever you like. Write. Read. Nap. Lounge. Wear a mantilla and danth the flamenco. No, a gypsy kerchief over your hair and gold hoops dangling from your ears.

LOUISE: I could tell fortunes and scare the hell out of everybody.

KEN: You'd look just like Marlene Dietrich in *A Touch of Evil*.

LOUISE: That galloping cow? No thanks, darling.

KEN: Why do you say that?

LOUISE: Well, for one thing, she said to all the papers "Imagine Georgie Pabst choosing Louise Brooks for Lulu when he could have had me." Oh, she was a bitch.

KEN: She's actually a dear friend of mine, darling.

LOUISE: Isn't the world of famous people small? Everybody knows everybody.

     Pause.

LOUISE: So. What did you do with her? Talk?

     Pause.

KEN: We disappeared for three days together.

     Pause.

LOUISE: Did you do it?

KEN: None of your business, darling.

LOUISE: Fuck you.

     They smoke.

LOUISE: Truth or Dare?

KEN: Dare.

LOUISE: Thought so.

KEN: So, what's the dare?

LOUISE: I'm sorry , darling, but the game is over for me once you state your preference.

KEN: All right. Truth, then.

LOUISE: Too late. *(Pause.)* You try me now.

KEN: But I know what you're going to say.

LOUISE: Try me. I might surprise you.

KEN: Well, then. Truth or Dare?

LOUISE: Truth.

KEN: You see?

LOUISE: Go ahead. Ask me anything.

KEN: Really?

LOUISE: Anything. Shoot.

          Pause.

KEN: I can't think of anything.

LOUISE: It's a good thing I didn't grant you three wishes.

KEN: All right. No matter how personal?

LOUISE: Anything.

KEN: You don't have to answer.

LOUISE: I will.

KEN: Do you ever have…do you have any…fantasies?

LOUISE: Fantasies.

KEN: You know. Of a…sexual nature.

LOUISE: No.

KEN: No?

LOUISE: Never.

KEN: Never.

LOUISE: Well, I never needed any, did I?

KEN: How interesting.

LOUISE: You?

KEN: Of course. I'm Kenneth Fucking Tynan, darling. I'm the man who said "fuck" on TV.

LOUISE: Now don't be like that.

KEN: Sorry.

              Pause.

KEN: You really trust me to write about you?

LOUISE: You are the only one I trust.

KEN: I'm really hopeless these days.

LOUISE: Oh, give me a deadly sin any day over insipid Hope.

KEN: The blancmange of human emotion.

LOUISE: I used to be quite an expert in sin, darling. Back before you were born. Now, let's see. Jealousy, avarice, greed...

KEN: Those two are the same. Covetousness.

LOUISE: Oh, right. Gluttony. Anger. Is anger one?

KEN: I think it is.

LOUISE: Sloth. Look out for that one, darling. Envy. No, we had...

KEN: ...had that one. Pride.

LOUISE: That one's for me. One, two, three, four, five, six. There's one…

KEN: Starts with an "L".

LOUISE: Oh! Love!

KEN: Lust.

LOUISE: Whatever. You know, I don't think I loved any man. It was easy to give them up for the public library.

KEN: Ha.

LOUISE: I used to know lots of brilliant, brilliant men. I never found any show business person as sexually attractive as a really brilliant literary mind, you know what I mean? That's what I find really—oh, glamorous. I just don't get to meet brilliant people any more.

KEN: Is that so?

LOUISE: I miss that most of all.

KEN: I could introduce you.

LOUISE: You could, couldn't you?

KEN: Yes.

LOUISE: After the thing comes out.

KEN: Of course. Who would you like to meet?

LOUISE: Who do you know?

KEN: Well, everybody.

LOUISE: Such as?

KEN: I introduced Tennessee Williams to Ernest Hemingway and Fidel Castro.

LOUISE: Well, I'm so fucking impressed, darling, I can't tell you.

KEN: It's true.

LOUISE: Did I say it wasn't?

KEN: I know some people in Los Angeles who would love to meet you.

LOUISE: I think that California sun fries the brain. You should get out of there while you can. Move to New York. That's where you belong. You could be my manager. What do you think? You're the only one who could manage me.

KEN: The climate here is terrible for my bronchitis.

LOUISE: Look, I've got emphysema and I'm fine. *(She watches him open his cigarette case.)* You should really give that up, sugar. No, I mean it. First day of the rest of your life or whatever.

KEN: The effort of the resolution would leave no time or energy for anything else.

LOUISE: I'm supposed to quit, you know.

KEN: Occupational hazard, darling.

LOUISE: This could be our last cigarette, right here.

KEN: I can just see the firing squad.

LOUISE: Picture me, blindfolded, hands tied, up against the wall.

KEN: Hmm.

LOUISE: Now stop! Your dirty mind!

KEN: Any last requests?

LOUISE: Have a light, darling?

They light up.

LOUISE: So, what do you say?

KEN: Maybe after I finish the article.

LOUISE: Promise me you will.

KEN: I will if you do.

LOUISE: When the article comes out.

KEN: Yes.

LOUISE: When's that?

KEN: Late spring.

LOUISE: This spring?

KEN: Seventy-nine.

LOUISE: That's over a year! Oh, that's fine. I can do it by then. Either that or I'll be dead. Now there's an idea. Could you write about me as if I were dead?

KEN: What about absolute truth and integrity? *(He gets up and picks up the phone.)*

LOUISE: What are you doing?

KEN: I have to get a cab. My plane leaves...

LOUISE: Get back over here, this instant. Come on. Sit here by me. Come sit next to Brooksie. *(He does.)* Look at those lovely hands.

KEN: *(Admiring them himself.)* Yes, they're very tenuous.

LOUISE: What a thing you are. Like a lovely peacock, all flash and crow.

KEN: Peacock is my middle name, darling.

LOUISE: Oh, I didn't mean it as an insult, darling, I meant… lovely things.

KEN: No, no. I mean Peacock is my actual middle name.

LOUISE: Oh. How truly bizarre. Maybe I'll change my name. What do you think? I can start over. How about June Caprice? That's good. Or Louise Lovely? Too vain. How about Lou Brou? Kind of Chinese.

KEN: Very Zen, darling.

LOUISE: Will you miss me when I'm gone?

KEN: Oh. Oh, of course. It'll be like losing a bit of myself.

LOUISE: But a little bit of me and you will always be together.

KEN: Yes.

LOUISE: In print. Where it counts. Where it lasts.

KEN: Yes.

LOUISE: What will you call it?

KEN: *(He touches her face as if drawing on Lulu's hair.)* "The Girl in the Black Helmet."

LOUISE: I like that. You understand me. I don't know if you know that, but I think you really do. Read to me, darling, before you go.

KEN: What shall I read?

LOUISE: *(Reaching for a book.)* This, this.

LOUISE opens the book to the right page. KEN puts his arm around her and she snuggles up with her head on his chest. LULU enters, smoking, drinking, dressed in a long black negligee, an angel of death. She remains in the background.

KEN: "My love is as a fever, longing still
For that which longer nurseth the disease;
Feeding on that which doth preserve the ill,
The uncertain sickly appetite..."

LOUISE: Go on. I didn't tell you to stop.

KEN: "...the uncertain sickly appetite to please.
My reason, the physician to my love,
Angry that his prescriptions are not met..."

Oh, darling, I'm sorry, this is a bit much for me right now.

LOUISE: Go on.

KEN: Er..."desire is death..."oh, dear..."past cure...
And frantic-mad with evermore unrest,
My thoughts and my discourse as madmen's are,
At random from the truth vainly express'd.
For I have sworn thee fair and thought thee bright,
Who art as..."

LOUISE: Oh, darling.

KEN: "Black as hell, as dark as night."

LOUISE: Lovely. Don't go.

KEN: I'll stay as long as you like.

KEN strokes her hair as LOUISE falls asleep.

KEN sits with LOUISE in his arms until he is sure she is asleep. He deliberates, then kisses her on the mouth. She remains asleep. He rises, tucks her into bed, and turns to LULU. She doesn't look at him.

KEN: Look at you. You're radiant.

LULU: I'm drunk, darling. I'm drunk.

KEN: Let us always be drunk, darling. We shall sit in this room and be drunk and radiantly beautiful forever, living on wine and bread, and black coffee.

LULU: But you don't like your coffee black, darling.

KEN: But it looks divine.

LULU: Too, too divine. These books, this music. We'll be so terribly Bohemian.

KEN: We'll live outside time. We will be always together, aspiring to be wonderfully alone.

LULU: We'll be perfectly unnatural.

KEN: Ordinary life is not our kind of thing. There will be no two—

LULU: No ones.

KEN: No two ones like us in history. Two beautiful, brilliant ones.

LULU: Sad. Careless.

KEN: Sad, careless radiant stars. Tragic.

LULU: B-but we won't know we're in a t-tragedy. We'll be alive like anyone else, buying groceries, making a meal, reading a book.

KEN: That, darling, is the tragedy. We won't know that we're
         living the same lives as boring, talentless, ordinary
         people.

LULU: We must try to forget them.

KEN: It will be very hard. Useless lives. Wasted lives. I'm
         terribly frightened of that kind of life. So we must
         squeeze life and enlightenment and pleasure out of every
         moment.

LULU: Darling.

KEN: I think I…

LULU: Yes, darling?

KEN: I'm going to say something important.

LULU: I'm ready, darling.

KEN: I think I could become very fond of you.

LULU: Nonsense, darling. It's just that my teeth match your
         wound.

> *LULU drops her cigarette into her glass, and exits.*

FILM:
Lulu's death scene from *Pandora's Box*.

Film synopsis: Lulu jumps into the lap of Jack
the Ripper. She playfully defends herself from
his kiss. She begins rummaging in his pockets,
and he lets her. She finds a sprig of mistletoe,
and a candle. She hunts around for a match and
lights the candle, then arranges the mistletoe
before it. She comes back into his arms. They
sit quietly. He suddenly picks up the mistletoe
and holds it over her head. "Now you must let
yourself be kissed."

She willingly shuts her eyes and raises her face. The sudden flare of a lamp catches his attention, and he sits frozen with horror as he sees the glint of a breadknife on the table. He shakes and struggles for breath, but cannot resist. He takes the knife.

Lulu waits for her kiss. She suspects nothing. Her lips part. The man leans over her, her head and hand can just be seen behind the man's broad back. There is a sharp movement, her hand stiffens, loosens, and falls.

The film clip plays as KEN *removes his jacket, unfolds a folding chair in the spotlight down centre where he began, and sits, alone. He looks very old and ill. He is not smoking.*

LULU *enters with a portable oxygen tank. She puts the clear blue plastic air tubing over his head with the cannula leading into his nostrils, running down to the tank. She reaches over his shoulders to tighten the tubing at his neck, like a necktie. She kneels at his feet and looks up at him.*

KEN: I did renounce the world in favour of a worthless thing. A mistress, so elegant, so sublime, so demanding. So faithful to me, so intolerant of anything that was not her.

This is my last cigarette.

It's a very inferior brand. I bought it from a crooked cardiac patient for an exorbitant sum. How unfair that this should be the last. Its taste erases all the lovely ones before.

(Caressing the handle of the oxygen tank.) Isn't this obscene? It's even rather disgusting to me now. But I've been forbidden, so I must.

You understand.

> *KEN bends down as LULU gives him a light. He smokes, painfully. Each drag burns his lungs, and he rubs his chest.*

You were so slender, so firm, with your paper-white skin, your smoldering eyes. The more I yield to you, the more you arouse me. My passion for you numbs my desire for anything else.

> *LULU places her head on KEN's lap.*

I wish I had a dozen of you in a platinum case. Multiples of you. Lined up absolutely. Restrained with a clip. A sublime row of chorus girls, each identical, each one ready for me, begging to be the one I'll choose, the one I'll caress. The one I'll ignite, destroy, ingest.

> *KEN considers the cigarette, the lifeless LULU, the audience.*

How poignant our short time together. How significant these five minutes of intimacy. How delightful to have killed a little time with you.

> *Lights fade. Film clip ends as Lulu's hand falls from Jack's shoulder. Blackout.*

THE END